RHYTHM IN 5

Nicola Cantan

Colourful Keys Books

Published in the Republic of Ireland

First Printing, 2019

ISBN 978-1-913000-10-3

Colourful Keys
78 Durrow Road
Dublin, D12 V3A3

www.vibrantmusicteaching.com

RHYTHM IN 5

Nicola Cantan

NICOLA CANTAN is a piano teacher, author, blogger and creator of imaginative and engaging teaching resources. She loves getting piano students learning through laughter and exploring the diverse world of music making through improvisation, composition and games.

Nicola's membership site, *Vibrant Music Teaching*, is helping teachers all over the world to include more games and off-bench activities in their lessons, so that their students giggle their way through music theory and make faster progress.

Nicola also runs a popular blog, *Colourful Keys*, where she shares creative ideas and teaching strategies, and hosts regular training events for piano teachers.

*To all students and teachers who have
ever been bored by clapping drills.*

CONTENTS

A Word of Caution

Do not read this book.

Sorry, let's try that again. Ahem. Do not READ this book.

Still unclear. One more go? Do not *only* **READ** this book.

Let me explain. What I don't want you to do is read this book the whole way through, in one go, without taking action on the ideas.

Because, first of all, that would be a pretty boring experience. This book is essentially all about movement. While the directions and descriptions are as clear and as entertaining as it's possible to make them, it's not exactly a gripping thriller. I doubt you'll be on the edge of your seat, and you'll probably sleep just fine tonight.

Nonetheless, I hope you'll be inspired by these activities. But that will only happen if you use the ideas with your students. That brings me to the second reason you shouldn't simply *read* this book: because that would be useless. The book is just a book. Just words on a page. If you read it without moving, chanting, playing and laughing with your music students, it will do exactly nothing.

So read, but don't forget to *do*.

THE RHYTHM PROBLEM

Do your students all play with excellent rhythm without much guidance from you? Do they value rhythm as much as they should, or do they sacrifice rhythm in favour of correct pitch?

If we think about it, we know that's not the right way round. In fact, if you or your students are not convinced of how vital rhythm is to music, I've got a fun little experiment for you to try.

- Play any famous melody (a folk song, perhaps, or a theme from a well-known classical piece) with completely incorrect rhythm, wildly off what it should be, but with all the correct notes.
- Now play the same tune with the correct rhythm, but mess up several of the pitches.

Which one sounded more like the actual music? The one with the correct rhythm, right?

It's remarkable the difference good rhythm makes. And, yet, many teachers (not pointing any fingers here) spend a curiously small portion of their lesson time working on rhythm. We often start pieces by focusing on the notes first and "fixing" the rhythm later.

No wonder our students don't place enough importance on rhythm. We're literally putting other things first.

But, with just a few minutes of lesson time, we can make a radical difference to our students' rhythm skills and literacy. We can guide our students to understand rhythms and rhythm notation better, which will help them play more fluently and, ultimately, more musically.

The investment is surely worth it.

WHY 5 MINUTES?

Because that's all we've got.

When I thought about writing this book, I considered what it was that was holding teachers back from passing on great rhythm skills to their students.

One element is that there simply aren't many resources dedicated to working on rhythm in one-on-one or small groups. Most books and courses are directed towards classroom teachers.

But the other part, and the biggest roadblock for most private teachers, is time. Most of us see our students once a week for 30-60 minutes. In that time, we need to review old repertoire, introduce new repertoire, teach practice techniques (like those found in another book of mine, *The Piano Practice Physician's Handbook*), drill scales and other technical exercises, work on aural skills, possibly do written theory work, and so much more.

So, I knew if I was going to make a difference for you, I needed to keep it snappy. Each of these activities actually could be done in as little time as 3 minutes, or extended to 10 minutes if you use the variation ideas. ("Rhythm in 3-10 Minutes" wasn't quite as catchy a title, so I decided to stick with 5.)

If you have trouble sparing even 3 minutes from your lesson I have two suggestions that will help.

The easiest way to make sure you get to something in your lessons is to start with it. Plan one of these rhythm games as a warm-up to do as soon as your student walks in the door.

Another great way to fit in these rhythm games is to use them as a brain break. Young students can concentrate much better if they get up and move every so often. Do one of these activities halfway through the lesson and, I promise, you'll get more done because your student will focus better after they've had a chance to wiggle a bit.

Oh, and if you have trouble fitting in the planning time outside of lessons? Use the same activity for every student in a week. They all work on multiple levels so you can use all 25 different games with 25 different students in one week. But why not make it easy for yourself? Just pick one at a time.

How this Book Works

Each exercise in this book includes the following:

- What are we learning here?
- The Basics
- Next Levels
- More Moves
- Instrumentation & Experiments

These sections will take you through the learning objectives for the game, clear instructions on how to do it, how to take it a step further, variations using body percussion and movements, and how to bring the exercise on to percussion or your own instruments and get creative with it.

The rhythm games have been laid out in this book in a rough order of difficulty. However, essentially, all the exercises are at the same level. A beginner can do any of these games with a teacher to guide them, and even an advanced student can learn something from the "next level" ideas for the exercises.

The activities in this book have been designed to require very little equipment and minimal prep time. However, there are three resources that are used throughout the book: *Rhythm Vocab, Relative Rhythms* and *Jumbo Note Values*. You can download all of these at vibrantmusicteaching.com/rhythmin5 and print them at home.

RHYTHM SYSTEMS

All of the exercises are designed to be done with rhythm syllables rather than metric counting (although one game, *Count Teddy*, does work on preparing students for metric counting). I have found that this is a much more natural, intuitive and effective way to work on rhythm with young students than starting metric counting right away.

If you already have a rhythm syllable system that you're comfortable with, such as Kodály or Takadimi, feel free to stick to that and adapt these activities to suit. If you don't have one already at your fingertips, try using my favourite, which is a modified version of Kodály.

♪	ka		♪♪♪ (triola)	triola		𝅝	ta-2-3-4
♫	tika		♩	ta		𝄼	kas
♪	ti		♩.	tum		𝄾	tis
♫	titi		𝅗𝅥	ta-2		𝄿	tas
♪.	tim		𝅗𝅥.	ta-2-3		−	tas-2

However unfamiliar you might be with using a rhythm system like this, I strongly encourage you to give it a go. It was a bit foreign to me once too, but I have seen much better results from working in this way, and starting with rhythm syllables of some sort is now recommended by many leading pedagogues all over the world.

THE MICRO-REVOLUTION

The exercises in this book are not revolutionary. You may have used some, or perhaps even all, of these rhythm activities before. Some are my own inventions but some are as old as the hills, so old that they exist in the ether, or feel like simple common sense.

The exercises in this book are not revolutionary. But they might start a micro-revolution in your studio.

Working on rhythm in a focussed way, even for just a few minutes out of every lesson, might just make all the difference for your students. It might mean you no longer have to badger students to *please count* or it might mean that you no longer have to teach rhythms by rote, because your students will understand them much more thoroughly.

My goal with this book is to help you:

- Work on rhythm more consistently with your students
- Add more variety to your rhythm work and make it an exciting part of the lesson
- Have more opportunities to explore and create with your students

I hope you'll have fun with these activities and games and that they start a micro-revolution in your studio. If they do, or if you have questions, I'd be delighted to hear from you. Just email me at nicola@vibrantmusicteaching.com. I get a lot of emails so I won't always respond right away, but I do personally read and value every single one.

And, if you want more support, access to the videos for all of these rhythm games, and a wealth of other courses, games and resources for music teachers, then I'd love to welcome you to the Vibrant Music Teaching community. You can find out more about it and sign up at vibrantmusicteaching.com/join

SWITCH-SWITCH

WHAT ARE WE LEARNING HERE?

This exercise is a great way to introduce a new note value, subdivision or metre. It also helps students to understand and feel a steady, consistent tempo. You take the lead, so even if a student is a bit out of time in the beginning they'll soon catch on as you switch, switch, switch, switch!

THE BASICS

- Start with *ta* and *titi* using patsch (tap hands on knees/lap) for both.
- Demonstrate *ta* and get your student to try it with you: "Let's do *ta* together!"
- Demonstrate *titi* and get your student to try it with you: "Let's do *titi* together!"
- Now tell them that you're going to start with *ta* and switch to *titi*.
- Start off together by saying "1 2 rea-dy go!" and patsch *ta* together. Once *ta* is firmly established say "1 2 rea-dy switch!" and change to *titi*.
- Switch back and forth several times. The goal is for your student to switch straight away, without faltering, but this can take time and may need to be repeated at several lessons.
- Always do the switch at the end of a bar/measure. (You'll probably do this instinctively.)
- Do the exercise saying the *ta* and *titi* aloud and

then try telling your student to just think them.

NEXT LEVELS

I've given the example of *ta* and *titi* above, but this exercise can be done with any pair of note values. After *ta* & *titi* try progressing to these combinations:

1. Ta-2 & ta
2. Ta-2 & titi
3. Ta & tikatika
4. Titi & tikatika
5. Ta-2 & tikatika
6. Ta-2 & tum-ti
7. Ta & tum-ti
8. Titi & tum-ti
9. Ta & triola
10. Ta-2 & triola
11. Titi & triola
12. Ta-2 & ti-ta-ti
13. Ta & ti-ta-ti
14. Titi & ti-ta-ti

To emphasise the relative nature of different note values, try doing fast *ta-2* & *ta*, followed by slow *ta* & *titi*. The difference is simply in the notation. This is especially useful for those students who think ♫ means play as fast as possible!

MORE MOVES

You can try lots of different combinations of movements for *Switch-Switch*. Try using clap for the longer note and patsch for the shorter note, jumps for the longer note and stamps for the shorter note, or tapping your head for the longer note and your shoulders for the shorter note.

It doesn't have to stop there either. Ask your student for some action suggestions and get really creative!

Instrumentation & Experiments

Once your student is used to the body percussion version of *Switch-Switch* try using some rhythm instruments to take the feeling of the note values into a new context.

Take this exercise into your other work at your instrument too and get your student to play scales or other simple exercises they're working on, switching back and forth between the note values at your instruction.

SWAP-SWAP

WHAT ARE WE LEARNING HERE?

Swap-Swap builds an understanding of how different note values relate to one another. Through this exercise, students will gain confidence in feeling various note values at any tempo. It's also fantastic practice for duet and ensemble work as they need to listen and tap at the same time.

THE BASICS

- Start with *ta* and *titi* using clap for *ta* and patsch for *titi*.
- Demonstrate *ta* and get your student to try it with you: "Let's do *ta* together!"
- Demonstrate *titi* and get your student to try it with you: "Let's do *titi* together!"
- Now tell them that you're going to start with *ta* and they're going to start with *titi*. When you say so, you'll swap with each other.
- Start off clapping and saying "1 2 rea-dy go!" If they have trouble finding the *titi* against your *ta* try saying *titi* while still clapping *ta*.
- Swap back and forth several times. The goal is for your student to swap straight away, without faltering, but this can take time and may need to be repeated at several lessons.
- Always do the swap at the end of a bar/measure. (You'll probably do this instinctively.)
- Do the exercise saying the *ta* and *titi* out loud

and then try telling your student to just think them.

- If you have multiple students you can do this by splitting them into two teams. As students get used to the exercise you can take yourself out of the picture and have the teams of students do it by themselves.

NEXT LEVELS

I've given the example of *ta* and *titi* above, but this exercise can be done with any pair of note values. After *ta* & *titi* try progressing to these combinations:

1. Ta-2 & ta
2. Ta-2 & titi
3. Ta & tikatika
4. Titi & tikatika
5. Ta-2 & tikatika
6. Ta-2 & tum-ti
7. Ta & tum-ti
8. Titi & tum-ti
9. Ta & triola
10. Ta-2 & triola
11. Titi & triola
12. Ta-2 & ti-ta-ti
13. Ta & ti-ta-ti
14. Titi & ti-ta-ti

If you are working with multiple students you can include more than just two note values and create *Swap-Swap-Swap* or *Swap-Swap-Swap-Swap* by rotating them around in a circle.

MORE MOVES

Come up with as many different combinations of movements as you can. Try clapping, patching, stamping, nodding, jumping and touching your toes. You could even use simple dance steps such as a waltz step for *triola* against marching for *ta*.

Instrumentation & Experiments

Bring some rhythm instruments into *Swap-Swap* to practise in a new context. Take these rhythms onto your instrument and play any two complementary notes or chords while swapping rhythms back and forth. You could also extend this into improvised duets by combining an accompaniment pattern and a scale using the rhythms you've been practising.

ECHOES

WHAT ARE WE LEARNING HERE?

Echoes is a great way for your students to build up a vocabulary of common rhythm patterns. By repeating short phrases and then creating their own they learn how different patterns feel without having to analyse notation. This is all about sound, not symbol or label.

THE BASICS

- Say a rhythm pattern and gesture for your student to join in on the echo. For example, you say "ta titi ta titi" pointing first to yourself and then to your student.
- Start with one bar/measure rhythms in 2/4 using only ♩ and ♫ Then extend these patterns to one bar/measure rhythms in 4/4 still using only ♩ and ♫

NEXT LEVELS

Begin to include other note values and work in other metres as your student is ready. When your student has a wider vocabulary within the one bar/measure structure extend the phrases to 2, 3 and 4 bars/measures to gradually build their aural memory.

MORE MOVES

A great way to improve your student's coordination and also make it easier to remember longer rhythms is to include different actions for each note value. Here are my favourites for each but feel free to adapt it to suit you and your students:

- ♫ = patsch twice
- ♩ = clap
- ♩ = clap-chop
- 𝄽 = touch shoulders

INSTRUMENTATION & EXPERIMENTS

Play tuned or untuned percussion or your instrument while saying and echoing the rhythm patterns. Pick two complementary notes since you'll be playing at the same time. (Stick to the percussion if you play an instrument where it's impossible to talk and play at the same time!)

COPYCAT

What are we learning here?

Copycat will help your students to grow their confidence by performing rhythms independently. Gradually, they will build up a feel for these simple rhythms so that when they see the notation the patterns feel like old friends.

The Basics

- Clap a simple rhythm and ask your student to copycat it back to you. Repeat this several times.
- Now ask your student to clap a rhythm for you to copycat.
- Swap roles back and forth. Encourage your student to keep their rhythm simple.

Next Levels

Most people (even music teachers!) will instinctively start with one bar/measure rhythms in $\frac{4}{4}$ time. As your student gets comfortable with the *Copycat* exercise try doing it in $\frac{3}{4}$ or $\frac{6}{8}$ time. Stick to one time signature in each session so that your student starts to pick up and mimic the feel of that metre. Once your student is familiar with each time signature and is successfully copying your patterns, extend the rhythms to two or more bars/measures to increase their aural memory and rhythm vocabulary.

More Moves

Copycat doesn't have to be just clapped. You might like to try stamping the rhythms or even combining different body percussion actions as your student progresses. For example, your student could patsch a rhythm and you stamp it back to them or you could clap a rhythm and they could nod it back to you.

Instrumentation & Experiments

Try doing these rhythms on your instrument using any notes or chords. You can let your student pick what notes they use to play the rhythm, helping them to distinguish between the concepts of rhythm and pitch.

Q&A

WHAT ARE WE LEARNING HERE?

By creating rhythm "questions" and "answers" students learn about musical phrases and the repetitive nature of music. This can help them as they compose their own music, and can also help them to better understand why the repertoire they are learning was composed in the way that it was.

THE BASICS

- Clap a simple rhythm – this is your "question".
- Ask your student to answer it with a similar rhythm. Repeat this several times.
- Now ask your student to clap a rhythm question for you to answer.
- Swap roles back and forth. Encourage your student to keep their rhythm simple.

NEXT LEVELS

As your student gets used to this format, start trying different time signatures and phrase lengths. Notice whether they follow you or mimic parts of your pattern in their answers.

Take this a step further by having your student notate their favourite rhythm question and answer. They could even use this as the start of a new composition.

More Moves

Combine stamping, clapping, patsching and jumping in your questions and answers. Stick with one note value for each action. For example ♫♩ ♫♩ might become: "stamp stamp clap stamp stamp clap". This can help students to latch on to the pattern and create their own to match.

Instrumentation & Experiments

Try doing *Q&A* with two different percussion instruments or on two complementary notes on your instrument.

Identify the rhythm questions and answers in their repertoire together and try changing the answer to another possibility by writing it in above the staff. Do they prefer this version or the original?

MARCHING ORDERS

WHAT ARE WE LEARNING HERE?

Connecting note values with how they feel within different time signatures is a very important step. It helps students to understand how the same note value can act differently, and how it's all about the context. This exercise makes that idea accessible even to very young students.

THE BASICS

- Practise each of these note value actions with your student:
    - ♫♫ = tap your hands gently on your head
    - ♫ = run on tip-toe
    - ♩ = march
    - ♩ = high-knee march
    - 𝅝 = jump

- Put on some music in 𝄴 and hold up one *Jumbo Note Values* card at a time.
- Change note value every few bars/measures and do the actions together for whichever note value you're holding up.

NEXT LEVELS

Add in other time signatures as and when your student is ready. I suggest using the same actions for the beat and subdivisions. For example, in § march for ♩. and run on tip-toe for ♫♩

More Moves

If you want to vary the moves, try asking your students for suggestions. Discuss why certain actions will/won't work for certain note values. Try out their ideas to see if they can be done in time with the music.

Instrumentation & Experiments

Assign a different instrument to each note value. Figure out together what key the music is in so you can find the tonic and use this on any tuned instruments in your collection. Here's an example of how a student might rotate through different instruments based on which card you're holding up:

- ♬♬ = glockenspiel (D only)
- ♫ = orange (D) desk bell
- ♩ = tambourine
- ♩ = orange (D) boomwhacker
- o = cymbal

You could then try combining a couple of your student's favourites that they think fit best with the music.

RHYTHM RACE

WHAT ARE WE LEARNING HERE?

Being able to retain a rhythm pattern in the mind's ear (even for a moment) is the first step towards transcribing rhythms and internalising rhythm patterns. This fun game is a great way to work on aural memory, and also to get the wiggles out at the same time.

THE BASICS

- Get your student to draw 2 *Rhythm Vocab* cards at random. (You can use a particular selection of cards if you want to focus on certain note values.)
- Say each rhythm together and then place the cards in different spots around the room.
- Clap one of the rhythms and ask your student to run to the one you clapped.
- Get your student to draw 2 more *Rhythm Vocab* cards at random, say them together, and ask your student to choose 2 more spots for these.
- Now clap one of the four and ask your student to run to the one you clapped. Repeat this a few times.

NEXT LEVELS

You can add more and more *Rhythm Vocab* cards to choose from if four gets too easy. Build up to as many as you can and also try this with the next levels of the *Rhythm Vocab* cards as they're introduced.

MORE MOVES

Draw pictures (or ask your student to draw them) of stick figures doing various different actions, such as:

- Spinning around
- Putting one hand in the air
- Putting two hands in the air

- Jumping
- Dancing
- Sitting on the floor
- Kneeling
- Hands on hips

Place a different *Rhythm Vocab* card under each one of these pictures. Now your student must do the matching action to identify which rhythm you clapped.

INSTRUMENTATION & EXPERIMENTS

Rather than clapping the rhythm, try playing it on your instrument. Start off just playing one repeated note and then introduce melodies. You might even be able to think of famous melodies that use some of the rhythm patterns, and play those.

BLIND MIRROR

WHAT ARE WE LEARNING HERE?

Blind Mirror is a fantastic dictation/transcription exercise for beginners. It encourages them to truly listen to rhythms and analyse what is happening. Through this exercise students will increase their aural memory and also improve on their ability to clearly communicate a rhythm pattern so that their partner can transcribe it.

THE BASICS

- Split the *Relative Rhythms* cards in half.
- Sit back-to-back with your student with a pile of *Relative Rhythms* cards in front of each of you and some popsicle sticks or pencils to act as barlines.
- Tell your student to make a 2 bar/measure rhythm. You make one as well.
- When the rhythms are ready, take turns to clap your rhythm for each other.
- The other person then has to recreate this rhythm underneath their own. They can ask to hear the rhythm again as many times as they need to.
- When both you and your student are ready, you can go and look at each other's rhythms to see if they match. If there are differences, discuss where/how the miscommunication happened.
- If you're working with multiple students they

can create the rhythms (sitting back-to-back in pairs) and you can give helpful hints as they work.

Next Levels

You can specify the time signature to be used to give your student practice creating rhythms with the correct number of beats in each bar/measure. As your student gets good at transcribing, you can also increase the length of the rhythms, one bar/measure at a time.

More Moves

Instead of simply clapping the rhythm for their partner, students can choose different actions for the different note values. This can actually make it easier for the other person to work out and recreate the rhythm.

Instrumentation & Experiments

You can place tuned or untuned percussion beside each partner, or have them go to the instrument to play their rhythm each time it is requested. Just make sure they don't see their partner's rhythm on the way!

SNAKE

What are we learning here?

Rhythm syllables work best when students get lots of practice saying them with you so that they feel the beat and get used to chanting them rhythmically rather than just "saying" them. *Snake* provides plenty of opportunity for this and can also help students to learn to track music and build their concentration.

The Basics

- Decide on a time signature together.
- Use *Relative Rhythms* cards with popsicle sticks or pencils as barlines to create a giant rhythm snake on the floor together. Don't go in a straight line; twist, turn and spiral around the room.
- Stand at one side of the room and say the rhythm the whole way through together.
- Count in before you start and keep going even if your student falters. If they get completely lost you can go and point to where you are so that they can join back in.

Next Levels

Try doing this exercise with a metronome – let your student choose the tempo each time.

If your student is getting really confident and secure, try starting at different ends of the *Snake*. You can start at the end and do the rhythm in reverse while they start at the beginning, and vice versa. Did you finish at the same time?

You could even create a canon by starting 2 bars/measures after your student. If you have a group of students, get each to start 1 bar/measure after the last.

More Moves

I recommend starting the *Snake* with vocalisations alone. Then, when your student is tracking well and staying with you successfully, you can combine this with clapping, stamping, tapping your shoulders, or any other action.

Instrumentation & Experiments

For most instruments, it will be hard to keep a clear view of the floor *Snake* while also playing, so I suggest using rhythm instruments such as tambourines, maracas, finger cymbals, small drums and claves.

BEAT MY RHYTHM

WHAT ARE WE LEARNING HERE?

What is rhythm, anyway? That's one of the questions this game helps clarify.

By switching between rhythm and beat, students learn not just about this distinction but also about listening to and following a beat, the effect an unsteady beat has on rhythm, and how the tempo chosen affects the feel of a rhythm pattern.

THE BASICS

- Take 4 *Rhythm Vocab* cards and lay them out in a row.
- Practise clapping this rhythm together. Do it a few times until your student is confident with the pattern.
- Ask your student to patsch a beat. They can choose the tempo but it has to stay steady, like a ticking clock.
- Once their beat is established, clap the rhythm in time with their beat.
- If they stop or falter, stop clapping, help them to start their beat again and then start the rhythm again.
- If your student is doing well, ask them to get another beat going, this time at a different tempo.
- Once you have tried this exercise a few times, swap roles and start a beat for them to clap the

rhythm to. They will have already heard how the two fit together which should make it easier for them to clap in time.

Next Levels

As students progress to different levels of *Rhythm Vocab* cards, this activity can be repeated with the new rhythm patterns and in different time signatures. You might also like to try alternating beat subdivisions with the main beats, especially in compound time signatures. For example, the first time your student could tap the ♩. in ⁶⁄₈ and the next time they could tap the ♫♪

More Moves

Once your student is comfortable doing the rhythm or the beat, it's time to combine them! Try tapping the beat in one hand and then joining in with the rhythm pattern in the other hand. Make sure to try this with both left and right being the "beat hand".

If two handed *Beat My Rhythm* gets easy, move on to other combinations:

- March the beat and clap the rhythm
- Nod the beat and patsch the rhythm
- Clap the beat and tap the rhythm with one foot

All of these build not just rhythmic awareness but

coordination skills too, and good coordination is helpful for learning the technique of any instrument.

Instrumentation & Experiments

Boomwhackers, desk bells and other tuned percussion instruments are a great way to bridge the gap between rhythm drills and the instrument. Pick two complementary notes and make one the beat and the other the rhythm. You could try combining the notes of a particular chord so they are learning about harmony at the same time.

Beat My Rhythm is also a great exercise to use with scales. Try having your student play a scale with a steady beat while you play the rhythm you've been practising that day on a drum. Or, vice versa, have them apply the rhythm to their scale while you drum a steady beat.

ROTATE

WHAT ARE WE LEARNING HERE?

Rotate requires a lot of concentration and a rock steady pulse. By moving through different rhythm patterns students get to hear the relationship between different note values and how they layer on top of each other.

THE BASICS

- Get your student to draw 3 *Rhythm Vocab* cards at random. (You can use a particular selection of cards if you want to focus on certain note values.)
- Say each rhythm together and then place the cards in between you and your student to make a circle/triangle of cards.
- Tell your student you'll both start by clapping the rhythm closest to them and when you say "1 2 ready rotate!" you'll each change to the next rhythm in the circle, going clockwise. Point to each card in the order they will do them so that they're clear on the order.
- Now tell them they're going to do the same pattern as before, starting with the card closest to them, but you're going to start with the card closest to you. If they have trouble sticking with their rhythm while you clap something different, get them to say the rhythms as they clap.

NEXT LEVELS

You can increase the number of cards in the circle as your student gets good at this exercise. You can also do this with other levels of *Rhythm Vocab* cards as they progress through them.

MORE MOVES

Assign a different movement to each card. For example, clap card 1, patsch card 2 and tap your elbow for card 3. These actions will then stay with that card no matter who is doing it.

If your student has trouble focusing or really needs to burn some energy, you can also do this standing and literally rotate to stand in front of the cards as you switch between them.

INSTRUMENTATION & EXPERIMENTS

Paper cups work great as a simple rhythm instrument. Try doing *Rotate* by tapping cups on the floor/table and swapping cups each time you change rhythm.

Take *Rotate* onto your instrument by placing the cards on the music stand (in a line instead of a circle). Play single repeated notes or short simple melodies together as you rotate through the rhythms. A pentatonic scale would be best as it will always sound pretty good no matter the combinations!

TREE TIME

WHAT ARE WE LEARNING HERE?

Notes are all relative to each other. It can be misleading to talk about a note being "4 beats" or "1 beat" when what's really important is how they fit together. Rhythm trees are a great way to work on these relationships, and following this up by putting the note values into a piece of music can really help to solidify how they work in the student's mind.

THE BASICS

- Spread the *Relative Rhythms* cards in a loose pile.
- Ask your student to find a semibreve/whole note.
- Now ask them to find a minim/half note. How many of those will fit inside the semibreve/whole note?
- Create a rhythm tree together by asking questions like this and laying out the cards in this pattern:

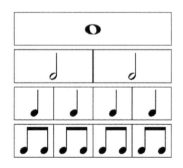

- Put a token (toy, eraser, pencil, etc.) beside one of the tree layers and tell your student you'll both patsch whichever note value this token is sitting beside.
- Put on some music in ¼ with a strong beat and patsch the note value together. Move the token every 4 bars/measures or so to practise the different note values.

Next Levels

Rhythm trees can be created starting with any note value at the top and going down as many layers as you like. Try making rhythm trees and doing *Tree Time* with different note and rest values and using different time signatures.

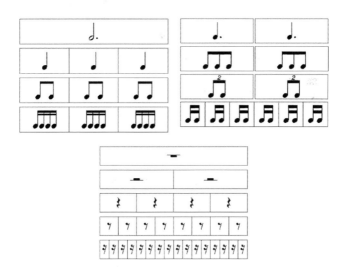

More Moves

Patsch is the easiest to start with but from there you can introduce clapping, tapping, marching and any other movements you like for *Tree Time.*

Instrumentation & Experiments

Choose a piece your student is currently working on and get them to try replacing all of a particular note value with a different note value of equal duration from the rhythm tree. For example, they could play their piece playing ♫♫ instead of ♩ – what effect does this have on the music? Do they like the original version better or this one?

GO, BLANK, GO!

WHAT ARE WE LEARNING HERE?

Inserting rests into a familiar rhythm pattern helps students learn to audiate rhythms and keep track of the beat. They also get a subliminal message about the importance of paying attention to, and counting during, rests.

THE BASICS

- Get your student to draw 6 *Rhythm Vocab* cards at random. (You can use a particular selection of cards if you want to focus on certain note values.)
- Place the cards in a row and clap the full rhythm together a few times.
- Have your student choose one card to be the "blank". Make sure you're both clear on which one it is but do not turn it over or remove it.
- Clap the rhythm together again but this time think this card rather than clapping it aloud.
- Repeat this as many times as your student needs in order to be able to start clapping again after the blank in time with you.

NEXT LEVELS

This exercise can be done with multiple "blank" cards and longer phrases. Try to build all the way up to twelve *Rhythm Vocab* cards with five blanks to keep track of!

MORE MOVES

Decide on a funny action to do during the blanks such as twirling around, high fiving or doing a jumping jack. This might seem like pure silliness (nothing wrong with that!) but it will help your student learn to multi-task by completing an action while still counting. This is a useful skill when they need to prepare for the next section during a rest or listen to an ensemble partner while counting their own part.

INSTRUMENTATION & EXPERIMENTS

Apply *Go, Blank, Go!* to your student's repertoire. Get them to choose a few bars/measures in their piece to think through rather than play. This is a great practice strategy to get them to focus at the same level for the entire piece, and to be able to pick up from any point.

WHO AM I?

WHAT ARE WE LEARNING HERE?

Who Am I? teaches students how note values can be transformed by other musical factors such as the time signature and the tempo. A ♩ in a funeral march is a very different thing to one in a fast toccata. This game allows them to feel and experience that difference.

THE BASICS

- Put one of the *Jumbo Note Values* cards in each corner of the room.
- Tell your student they should follow your lead and clap along with you. Afterwards, you'll ask which note value you were clapping so they should make sure to pay attention.
- Put on some music and clap together. Pause the music and tell them to run to the correct note value.
- Unpause the music once they have guessed correctly and repeat the activity a few times with different note values.

NEXT LEVELS

This game can be done with music in any time signature. You can even use repeated patterns of note values rather than single ones. For this, you would need to make your own rhythm pattern posters or simply have students tell you the answer instead of running to it.

More Moves

Who Am I? is a great one to get the wiggles out. Not only will students be running to the answer each time, but you can do any movement to demonstrate the note value. Try marching, doing jumping jacks, spinning around or doing a forward fold and slowly rolling up to standing (or quickly, depending on the note value – just watch out for head-rushes).

Instrumentation & Experiments

Rhythm instruments are a great addition to this game. You can use tambourines, jingle sticks, claves, finger cymbals or anything else you have around your studio to demonstrate the note values.

CLAP, TAP, THINK

WHAT ARE WE LEARNING HERE?

Being able to concentrate on two things at once, and *never* sacrifice the rhythm, is a very important skill for all musicians to develop. By building up a list of different actions and always being consistent with the rhythm, students will learn to divide their attention and multi-task.

THE BASICS

- Create a 4 bar/measure rhythm together using the *Relative Rhythms* cards. Use popsicle sticks or pencils as the barlines.
- Clap and say the rhythm together.
- Decide on one note value to turn into a tap and perform the rhythm again. For example, all ♩ are tapped but all other note values are still clapped.
- Now choose one note value that you will both think instead of making any sound and perform the rhythm again.

NEXT LEVELS

You can increase the length of the rhythm to make this game more challenging, and it can also be done with the *Rhythm Vocab* cards in place of the *Relative Rhythms* cards to add variety.

More Moves

You can add as many layers to this as you like. Just make sure to alter one note value at a time and not choose an action for each note value at the outset. The point of this exercise is to feel the rhythm in multiple ways. Here are some other actions you might try:

- Touch head
- Twirl
- Point to the sky
- Cross your arms
- Hands on hips
- Tap index fingers together
- High five
- Cover your eyes

Instrumentation & Experiments

Try whatever set of assigned note value actions you landed on with one of your student's pieces. Acting out their repertoire in this way can help them to connect more with a tricky rhythm, and to get to know and remember their piece more thoroughly.

WHAT DID I SAY?

WHAT ARE WE LEARNING HERE?

Setting words to rhythm is a very useful skill and something that's best introduced early in a student's learning. In this exercise, you're making the words rhythmic, so the student can then take them and make the connection to rhythm notation.

THE BASICS

- Spread out the *Relative Rhythms* cards in a loose pile.
- Clap and say a short rhythmic phrase. This can really be anything said as a chant, such as "Mississippi mud pie" or "mountain high, valley low". Choose words that will easily translate to note values your student knows. If you're stuck for inspiration, take phrases from kids' nursery rhymes and songs.
- Ask your student to recreate the rhythm with the *Relative Rhythms* cards.
- Clap and count the rhythm together, saying the rhythm syllables and then the words.

NEXT LEVELS

Using this format you can build up gradually to longer and longer phrases. You can also start to get your student to write the rhythm notation rather than using the *Relative Rhythms* cards, although the cards are best in the beginning to make the exercise accessible.

MORE MOVES

These rhythms will be pretty easy for your student to remember, so they're a great opportunity to get up and moving. Stamp out the rhythms, or try creating your own dance moves together based on the original words.

INSTRUMENTATION & EXPERIMENTS

If your student has a piece coming up with a particularly tricky rhythm, this exercise would be a great first introduction to the rhythm pattern in the piece before they even start work on it. Make up your own lyrics (if the piece doesn't already have them) and feed them to your student in short sections using this game. If you then get up and march, jump and stamp that rhythm while saying the words, your student will know it inside-out when they start work on the piece.

CANON

WHAT ARE WE LEARNING HERE?

It requires a lot of focus to be able to keep to your part while someone else does a contrasting rhythm. This exercise not only helps strengthen students' understanding and execution of the rhythm patterns, but it's a great preparatory exercise for working on ensemble pieces too.

THE BASICS

- Get your student to draw 6 *Rhythm Vocab* cards at random. (You can use a particular selection of cards if you want to focus on certain note values.)
- Place the cards in a row and say the full rhythm together a few times.
- Then tell your student to say the rhythm again but, this time, you're going to start 2 bars/measures after them to create a canon.
- If your student is able to stick with their rhythm successfully, swap roles and tell them to start 2 bars/measures after you.

NEXT LEVELS

Once your student gets good at vocalising rhythms in canon you can try clapping the rhythms instead. Encourage your student to say the rhythms in their head as they go so that they can stay on track.

You might also like to try setting words to the rhythm and trying that as a canon while clapping.

MORE MOVES

Canon rhythms can be practised with patching, clapping, tapping or stamping. Just make sure your student still has a clear view of the cards if you're moving around.

INSTRUMENTATION & EXPERIMENTS

Take the 6 *Rhythm Vocab* cards and place them on the music stand. Have your student start the rhythm with a scale or technical exercise they are working on, and then join in with the same scale and rhythm in canon. The rhythm can be repeated if needs be to get through the full scale.

Try different canon experiments with your student. What does it sound like if you start 1 bar/measure after them? 3 bars/measures? What about 5 notes, ignoring where they are in the bar/measure?

COORDINATION COMBOS

WHAT ARE WE LEARNING HERE?

Music students can sometimes struggle to grasp syncopated rhythms, two against three, or other such awkward combinations. When they have felt these rhythms against the beat, however, it makes it so much easier and more intuitive to play them on their instrument. *Coordination Combos* can take a while for students to get the hang of, but most will find the challenge fun.

THE BASICS

- First, practise the *syn-co-pa* or *ti-ta-ti* pattern ♪♩ ♪ as patsch-clap-patsch together.
- Then start marching a steady beat on the spot and try to add this rhythm pattern on top of your marching.

NEXT LEVELS

I've given the example of *ti-ta-ti* above, but this exercise is also great for feeling triplets, or any other tuplet or syncopation, really. It allows students to work on these counterintuitive combinations as a gross motor skill first so that they can more easily understand and apply it at their instrument.

More Moves

I recommend sticking with marching for the beat as this is the easiest to keep steady and combine with other movements. You can easily replace the patsch-clap-patsch pattern with any other body percussion you can come up with. Ask your students for suggestions and have fun with the more unusual combinations this results in!

Instrumentation & Experiments

Once your student has mastered the combination as a gross motor activity, you can apply this at your instrument using any scales or technical drills you're working on.

For pianists, try doing the beat in one hand against the syncopated or tuplet rhythm you've been working on in the other hand. For other instruments and voice, you (or another student if you teach in groups) can keep the beat while the student practises a scale or exercise in the new syncopated or tuplet rhythm.

UNJUMBLE

WHAT ARE WE LEARNING HERE?

Unjumble is an easy step towards rhythm transcription. By limiting the options of available rhythms in this game, we make it more likely that our students will be successful. But they still need to concentrate to remember the rhythm pattern and recreate it with the cards.

THE BASICS

- Get your student to draw 4 *Rhythm Vocab* cards at random. (You can use a particular selection of cards if you want to focus on certain note values.)
- Place the cards in a 2x2 grid.
- Choose a secret order for the cards and clap it for your student.
- It's your student's job to then put the cards in a row in the correct order. They can ask to hear the rhythm again as many times as they like.

NEXT LEVELS

To increase the difficulty, simply increase the number of cards your student will need to "unjumble". You can also start to specify the number of times you will clap the rhythm, for example clapping it 3 times before they can move any cards.

MORE MOVES

It's good for students to translate a variety of movements and vocalisations into rhythms. Try marching, tapping and saying the rhythm in any made-up syllables you can think of. Mix it up each time!

INSTRUMENTATION & EXPERIMENTS

You can also show the rhythm on any instrument instead of clapping it. Try using a single repeated pitch at first, and then make up melodies for the pattern so that your student has to listen out for just the rhythm. If you're a pianist, you could even put the rhythm in your left hand and play with your right hand in a different rhythm to try and "distract" your student.

Once your student has figured out the order of the rhythm cards you can also use this as a starting point for an improvisation or composition. Put them up on the music stand and tell your student to start with one repeated note for the complete rhythm, and to then incorporate neighbouring notes or other familiar patterns once they're used to the rhythm. You can play a simple accompaniment to provide richness and keep the beat going.

MY FAVOURITE THINGS

WHAT ARE WE LEARNING HERE?

Language is made up of all sorts of fantastic rhythms. *My Favourite Things* takes words your student knows and loves, and transforms them into a rhythm pattern to work on transcription and audiation.

THE BASICS

- Ask your student what their favourite dinner is. Say this a few times together rhythmically. Clap with each syllable.
- Ask your student what their favourite drink is. Say the drink name a few times together rhythmically. Clap with each syllable.
- Finally, ask your student for their favourite dessert. Say the dessert name a few times together rhythmically. Clap with each syllable.
- Now, combine their favourite things and chant this a few times while clapping. For example: "Pizza, apple juice and chocolate cake."
- Write this phrase down and help your student to work out what the rhythm is. Write the rhythm above the words. Depending on the student's age and level they might write this themselves or you might do it for them.
- Get your student to choose one favourite thing to eat/drink first. Clap and say the rhythm again but leave a rest where that item was.
- Get your student to choose another favourite

thing to eat/drink next. Clap and say the rhythm again but leave a rest where the two items were.
- The last time you do the rhythm, everything has been gobbled up! Count in and think the rhythm together, only clapping the "and".

Next Levels

You can apply this structure to any other topic; it doesn't have to be food. It could be your student's favourite sports, classes in school, composers, or the names of all their pets or family members.

You can also make the phrases longer by forming more complete sentences, such as: "On Monday I play basketball, Tuesday is tennis."

More Moves

Depending on what the favourite things are, you could come up with specific actions to match. For example, pizza might be a slicing motion, and for basketball you could dribble twice and then shoot. Being able to do these actions in time requires a good sense of pulse and feeling for the rhythm pattern.

Instrumentation & Experiments

These rhythms can make a great starting point for a composition. Take the rhythm you created together back to your instrument and have your student experiment with different melodies. This can open up a discussion about the articulation, dynamics and expression to represent their favourite things and will help to make these aspects of music feel more relevant for your student.

MEMORY TRAIN

WHAT ARE WE LEARNING HERE?

Short term recall can help students to internalise different rhythm patterns and create a rhythm vocabulary to draw from later. This makes reading new pieces easier as they will have already "met" some of the rhythms before. This is also a great tactic to break down a piece that a student needs to memorise.

THE BASICS

- Get your student to draw 4 *Rhythm Vocab* cards at random. (You can use a particular selection of cards if you want to focus on certain note values.)
- Place the cards in a row and clap and say the full rhythm together a few times.
- Now turn over the first card so that your student can no longer see the rhythm. Ask them if they can remember what it was. If they can't, show it to them again so they can look at it and memorise it, and then turn it back over.
- Clap and say the full rhythm together again.
- Turn over the next card and repeat the process until you're doing the whole rhythm from memory. Then ask them to clap it one final time, this time without saying it.

Next Levels

Get your student to do the rhythm train on their own once they're used to the process. You can just be the train driver and point to the cards as they say them rather than saying the rhythm with them.

If the *Memory Train* becomes easy, increase the number of carriages (cards) you use, and try turning over two at a time instead of just one.

More Moves

Once the full rhythm pattern is memorised, create a human rhythm train! March around the room with one person's hands on the other's shoulders and get the leader to run to the back at the end of each bar/measure. (If your student is small you may need to do this on your knees.)

Instrumentation & Experiments

Use this memorised pattern to improvise on your instrument. Experiment together using scales, arpeggios, consecutive thirds and other familiar patterns.

TWINS OR TRIPLETS

WHAT ARE WE LEARNING HERE?

Understanding metre is so much easier when you move to the music. Moving in this way can also change how your students feel about and express the time signature of the music they play when they analyse it in another person's playing.

THE BASICS

- First, practise these two patterns with your students:
    - Count "1 2 3" with the pattern clap-patsch-patsch
    - Count "1 2" with the pattern clap-patsch
- Go back and forth between these patterns until your student is really comfortable with them.
- Now put on some music in either duple or triple metre and ask your student to try both patterns and see which fits best. Does the music have twins or triplets hiding inside?
- Once they have discovered the correct answer explain what we call this metre and why it feels the way it does.

NEXT LEVELS

You can bring in quadruple metre (quadruplets!) once your student has a good grasp of duple and triple. For this, I like the pattern clap-touch shoulders-patsch-touch shoulders.

MORE MOVES

A great way to make it easier to relate to different metres and what they feel like is to teach your student some simple dance moves. You don't have to be an amazing dancer yourself to learn to waltz side to side or do a basic reel step on the spot.

INSTRUMENTATION & EXPERIMENTS

Take one of your student's pieces and work out together how you could change the metre. Have your student try playing a few bars/measures of their piece in a different metre. How does it change the piece? Do they like it more in the original time signature or the experimental one?

COUNT TEDDY

WHAT ARE WE LEARNING HERE?

While most of the exercises in this book focus on using some form of rhythm syllables, music students also need to understand and be able to use metric counting. This game works best as preparation long before they need to count out rhythms or count with their pieces, although it can also be done to help students who have already started to learn about metric counting.

THE BASICS

- Place the ♫ ♩ ♩ and ○ *Jumbo Note Values* cards on the floor in a row.
- Put a stuffed toy or teddy bear (I like to introduce him as *Count Teddy* or Count Oink, etc. depending on the type of toy) sitting on top of the ♩
- Count and patsch "1 2 3 4 1 2 3 4...".
- Now ask your student to move *Count Teddy* to another card. Tell them you're going to count out these note values and they should change it at some point during your counting to a different card again.
- Count and patsch the new note value and, when your student moves Count Teddy, finish out the bar/measure before changing to the new note value.

Next Levels

Count Teddy can be used to practise any note values in any time signature. Try moving to ¾ next, using the ♫♫ ♫ ♩ and ♩. *Jumbo Note Values* cards. Then move on to other time signatures, including compound ones. You might also like to show the time signature to your student as they get used to metric counting, although I recommend just letting them follow your lead in the beginning and connecting up the dots with the symbol later.

More Moves

Switching up the action each time can be lots of fun and keeps your student on their toes (perhaps literally!). Here are a few action suggestions that work well with *Count Teddy*:

- Patsch
- Clap
- March
- Touch head
- Twirl
- Hug yourself and unravel
- Hands on hips
- Tap index fingers together
- Twist side to side
- Sit down and stand up
- Sway from one foot to the other
- Swim your arms forward

Instrumentation & Experiments

You can transfer this exercise directly to your instrument using a single repeated note or scale. If it's awkward for your student to move *Count Teddy* when you're at your instrument (not a problem for voice teachers, but likely will be for most others) then try setting up several music stands, each with a *Jumbo Note Values* card on it, and asking your student to move to the one they want you to do next. If you need to sit to play your instrument, you could have your student place the *Jumbo Note Values* cards on the stand in the order that they want you to move through them before you begin playing. And if you're playing a wind instrument you may need to forgo the counting or set up a metronome app (some even count out loud) to do this for you.

DOUBLE BUBBLE

WHAT ARE WE LEARNING HERE?

In *Double Bubble,* students get first-hand experience of the fluid nature of note values. It's like they're participating in an experiment – like a chemistry experiment in school – to "prove" that the note values are all related and, in a way, interchangeable with each other.

THE BASICS

- Spread out the *Relative Rhythms* cards in a loose pile.
- Tell your student to make a short rhythm using only ♫ and ♩
- Ask your student which note is twice the size of ♩ Can they find one?
- Now ask your student which note is twice the size of ♪ Can they find one?
- Ask them to recreate the rhythm using ♩ and ♩ instead of ♫ and ♩
- Clap both rhythms together at fast, slow and medium speeds.
- Then tell your student you're going to clap one of them. Can they figure out which one it is?
- Clap the rhythm and talk about how there's no way to tell because it could be one of them at a fast tempo or the other one quite slow.

Next Levels

Try this exercise with lots of different note values in lots of different (implied) time signatures.

- ♪ and ♩ –> ♪ and ♩
- ♩ and ♩ –> ♩ and 𝅝
- ♫♩ and ♩. –> ♩ ♩ ♩ and ♩.

All of these can also be done in the reverse, getting your student to halve instead of double the note values.

More Moves

Try combining two different actions for these rhythms, keeping the effect the same in both versions. For example, in the first rhythm ♫ might be patsch-patsch and ♩ might be clap. Then in the second version, ♩ ♩ would be patsch-patsch and ♩ would be clap.

Instrumentation & Experiments

Have your student rewrite a short section of one of their pieces on a piece of manuscript paper using double or half notation. Ask them what else might need to change to keep the effect the same. Decide what the new time signature and tempo would be and write these in too.

LISTENING LOCOMOTIVE

What are we learning here?

Listening Locomotive helps students develop the skill of listening and playing at the same time, which is an important and sometimes difficult skill to pick up. This is useful not just for playing with other musicians, but also to allow your student to *really listen* to their own playing. Plus, they'll need to develop a rock steady beat to get really good at this one!

The Basics

- Start by clapping and saying a rhythm pattern and ask your student to join in and say it with you when they're ready.
- Stop the rhythm for a moment and explain that this time you'll start with this rhythm and change to a new rhythm pattern at some point. They need to try and keep the first rhythm pattern going while listening to your new pattern – once they feel like they've got it they should change to the new one.
- Don't worry if your student's transition to the new rhythm isn't very smooth when you first try this. Don't stop to correct them, just keep repeating the second rhythm until they catch on, then change to a new pattern again once they're confident with it.

Next Levels

This game will naturally get faster and faster as your student gets better at it. This keeps things interesting and keeps your student progressing nicely. You can incorporate new note values as they encounter them, but don't use this game to introduce a new note value. It's much more fun and educational when your student knows the note values being used very well already.

More Moves

You can absolutely use movements other than clapping for *Listening Locomotive* but try to stick to ones that are not too loud so your student can still hear you clearly. Patsching or tapping two fingers on your palm would work well.

Instrumentation & Experiments

This is a fantastic (and challenging!) game to play with scales and other technical exercises. Use one very simple rhythm pattern for the full scale/exercise. Demonstrate it for your student and then repeat it a few times together in this rhythm. Play the scale again, but this time you should change your rhythm to a new pattern while they keep theirs the same.

Then repeat the second rhythm with them now joining you in the new pattern. If they were listening well they should be able to play in time with you on the first try. If not, just repeat it a few times until they have the new rhythm – then change it again.

PURSUING YOUR RHYTHM REVOLUTION

At the beginning of this book, I talked about your micro-revolution. Can you feel the tides of revolution turning yet?

If you took my advice to take action as you go, you might have started to see the first shoots and sprouts of better rhythm skills in your students. If you haven't seen the effects yet even though you've been taking action (you haven't just been *reading*, have you? If so go back and read the introductory notes!) then keep at it.

Rhythm is a long game. You need to take little steps each and every week to make a difference. But, if you do, and if you stick at it, you'll look around one day and discover that rhythm is not a struggle for your students anymore. They'll be playing better, they'll be the most sought after ensemble, orchestra and band musicians of their age, and you'll be free of nagging about rhythm.

You'll be free to talk about the things you really want to talk about: the nuances of music, interpretation, expression and the backstories behind pieces, and free to just enjoy making music together.

These 25 rhythm games are just a starting point. Once you start working with rhythm in this way, and master and explore all of these exercises with your students, you'll start to come up with your own ideas and variations.

This is your own rhythm revolution in full swing. Embrace it and, please, share it with others. If you come up with your own rhythm game share it in the Vibrant Music Studio Teachers group on Facebook (all music teachers welcome!) or email me about it at nicola@vibrantmusicteaching.com.

Acknowledgements

I would like to thank every teacher I've had who has approached rhythm in a unique way. In particular, I'd like to thank Kodály Ireland, which provides fantastic training that has, in a very short time, had a strong influence on how I teach and think about rhythm.

Thanks are also due to the creators of the *Piano Safari* books, Katherine Fisher and Dr. Julie Knerr. The training they provide through their website and books is insightful, thoughtful and generous, and using their method is a great way to learn more about teaching rhythm.

Every teacher who shares their thoughts, knowledge and ideas online, whether through podcasts, blog posts or videos, is in a similar manner having a profound impact on the world of music teaching. Together, we're creating a generous community that embraces teachers of all backgrounds. Instead of closing our doors on one another and hiding our "secrets", I find more and more music teachers are saying, "Let me show you how I do it," and embracing the mantra of *community not competition*. I hope this attitude continues to spread.

Finally, and most importantly, I would like to thank my proofreader, Janine Levine. Without her, this entire book (including this acknowledgement to her!) would be a garbled mess.

INDEXES

INDEX BY CONCEPT

INDEX BY RESOURCES USED

More from Nicola Cantan

Thank you for reading *Rhythm in 5*. If you liked the book, please leave a review wherever you purchased it. I'd truly appreciate it. And if you're interested in more resources like this, you might also like these.

Vibrant Music Teaching

 *Vibrant Music Teaching* is the perfect resource to help you level-up your teaching and teach using more creativity. There is a library of video courses (including one to go with this book) and every printable game and activity you could need for your students.

To get more information and sign up for membership, go to: www.vibrantmusicteaching/join

The Piano Practice Physician's Handbook

 We all know a huge amount of the learning that needs to occur happens in the practice room, not the lesson room. This book (specifically for piano teachers, although many of the ideas can be adapted) will help you to help your students practice more effectively.

You can get it on Amazon or your favourite online or in-person bookshop.

Thinking Theory is a series of music theory workbooks designed to accelerate learning while providing plenty of reinforcement of each concept. All concepts are presented in a clear and concise way and page layouts are clean and consistent. No topic is introduced without being revisited several times later in the book.

Thinking Theory is designed in such a way that you can start anywhere in the series. Concepts already covered are not omitted from later books; they are just covered more briefly.

The workbooks incorporate solfa singing, rhythm work and carefully levelled theory concepts. Take a look, at: thinkingtheorybooks.com

COLOURFUL KEYS BLOG

Nicola writes regular articles and shares ideas on her blog, *Colourful Keys*. Check it out if you're looking for more piano teaching inspiration, at: www.colourfulkeys.com

Printed in Great Britain
by Amazon

66450804R00050